PAUL S. SCHUDER

Science Collections

Woodland Public Library

Mimbres design from Art of a Vanished Race

BURNING
AND MELTING

Design	David West
	Children's Book Design
Editor	John Clark
Picture researcher	Cecilia Weston-Baker
Illustrator	Ian Moores
Consultant	Alan Morton PhD
	Science Museum, London

First published in
the United States in 1990 by
Gloucester Press
387 Park Avenue South
New York NY 10016

Library of Congress Cataloging-in-Publication Data

Lafferty, Peter.
    Burning and melting : projects with heat / Peter Lafferty.
        p. cm. -- (Hands on science)
    Summary: Discusses heat, both as a natural phenomenon and as
an application in industry, and presents related projects.
    ISBN 0-531-17235-X
    1. Heat--Juvenile literature. 2. Heat--Experiments--Juvenile
literature. 3. Fusion--Juvenile literature. [1. Heat. 2. Heat-
-Experiments. 3. Experiments.] I. Title. II. Series.
QC256.L33 1990
536'.078--dc20   90-3222 CIP AC

HANDS · ON · SCIENCE

BURNING
AND MELTING

Peter Lafferty

GLOUCESTER PRESS
London · New York · Toronto · Sydney

CONTENTS

This book is about burning and melting — from how things burn to using fuels in engines. It tells you what heat is, and how it travels. There are "hands on" projects for you to try, which use everyday items as equipment. There are also quizzes for fun.

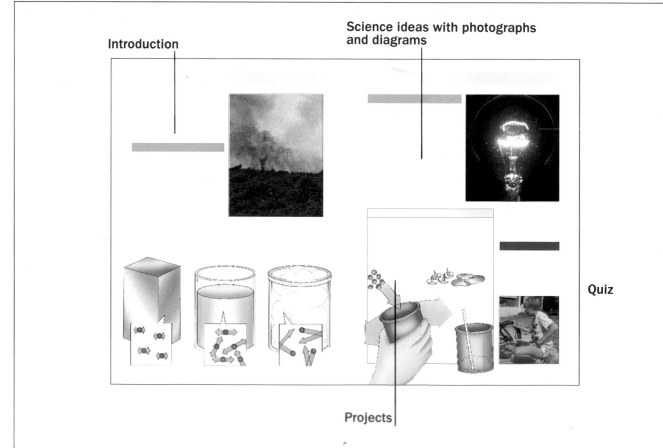

Introduction

Science ideas with photographs and diagrams

Quiz

Projects

INTRODUCTION

Heat is one of the essentials of life. People first learned to control heat when, long ago, they discovered how to use fire. The first fires people made were probably lit by snatching burning twigs from fires started by lightning. From then on, people could warm their homes and cook food. People also, after many thousands of years, began to learn about such things as extracting metals from ores. This was the beginning of chemistry — the science that studies chemical reactions. Burning was one of the earliest reactions studied by chemists. Other scientists studied the physical effects of heat, such as melting, evaporation, and expansion. By understanding these processes, scientists have been able to harness the energy of heat for an ever increasing number of useful purposes. It would be difficult to imagine life today without the many different ways we use heat — in industry, in transportation and in our homes.

The burning campfire provides the warmth necessary for life.

There is a difference between heat and temperature. The heat of an object is the total amount of energy it has because its molecules are moving. Moving molecules have kinetic energy. The temperature of the object indicates how fast the molecules are moving. The faster they move, the higher the temperature.

TEMPERATURE SCALES

There are three common temperature scales: Celsius (which is the same thing as centigrade), Fahrenheit and kelvin. On the Celsius scale, the temperature of freezing water is 0°C, and the temperature of boiling water is 100°C. On the Fahrenheit scale, freezing water is 32°F and boiling water is 212°F. Zero degrees in the kelvin scale is taken as the lowest possible temperature, called absolute zero, which is -273.15°C (-459.67°F). The size of a degree in the kelvin scale is the same as in the Celsius scale. So freezing water is 273.15 K.

△ An iceberg contains more heat than a cup of boiling water. Even though it is freezing, it is large and so its total energy is enormous.

▽ The hottest place on Earth is Al'Aziziyah in Libya. On September 13, 1922, a temperature of 58°C (136.4°F) was recorded.

INTRODUCTION

Heat is one of the essentials of life. People first learned to control heat when, long ago, they discovered how to use fire. The first fires people made were probably lit by snatching burning twigs from fires started by lightning. From then on, people could warm their homes and cook food. People also, after many thousands of years, began to learn about such things as extracting metals from ores. This was the beginning of chemistry — the science that studies chemical reactions. Burning was one of the earliest reactions studied by chemists. Other scientists studied the physical effects of heat, such as melting, evaporation, and expansion. By understanding these processes, scientists have been able to harness the energy of heat for an ever increasing number of useful purposes. It would be difficult to imagine life today without the many different ways we use heat — in industry, in transportation and in our homes.

The burning campfire provides the warmth necessary for life.

Nothing can move without energy, so it is lucky for us that energy comes in many forms. Heat is one form of energy. This is shown when a hot-air balloon rises in the sky. Heat energy makes the air in the balloon expand and so become less dense than the surrounding air. The balloon then floats.

MOVING MOLECULES

A hot object has energy because the tiny particles it is made of (atoms and molecules) are moving. If we touch the object, we feel the movement of the molecules as warmth or heat. In a solid, there are strong forces attracting each molecule to its neighbors, and so the molecules cannot move far. However, they are able to vibrate rapidly. In a liquid, the atoms and molecules can move more than in solids because the force between molecules is less strong. This is why a liquid can flow. In a gas, the force between molecules is weak and they can move freely. They bounce off the sides of their container.

△ A forest fire shows the power of uncontrolled heat. It causes great destruction, and its energy lifts vast amounts of smoke and ash into the air.

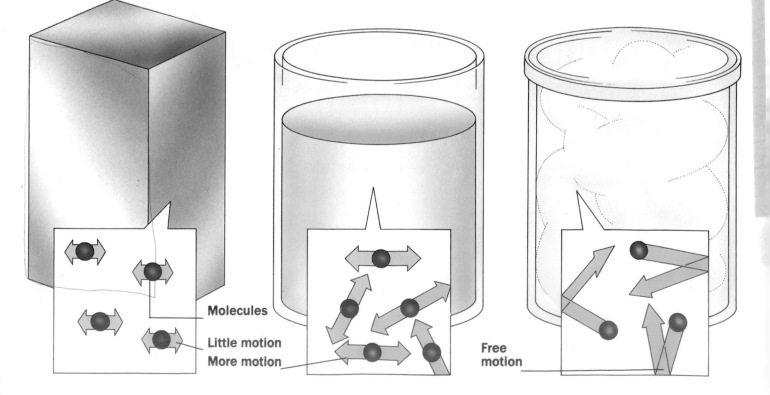

Solid   Liquid (in glass)   Gas (in sealed container)

Molecules

Little motion
More motion

Free motion

CHANGING ENERGY

There are many different forms of energy, including heat, light, electrical, sound, chemical, nuclear, stored (or potential) and movement (or kinetic) energy. Whatever its form, energy can be used to do work, such as lifting a weight. The units used to measure energy and work are called joules. A person who lifts a weight of 1 newton (about the weight of an apple) through a distance of three feet does 1 joule of work and at the same time uses at least one joule of energy.

One form of energy can be converted into a different form. For example, electrical energy can be converted into heat energy by an electric heater, or into kinetic energy by an electric motor.

△ Electricity produces heat and light in the filament of an electric lamp. The power of a lamp is measured in watts. A 100-watt lamp uses 100 joules of energy each second.

HOT SHOT

You can convert kinetic (or movement) energy to heat by shaking small metal balls in a cardboard tube. First measure the temperature of the balls using a thermometer. Then shake the balls vigorously. Measure the temperature again. It rises because the balls take up some of the energy of shaking.

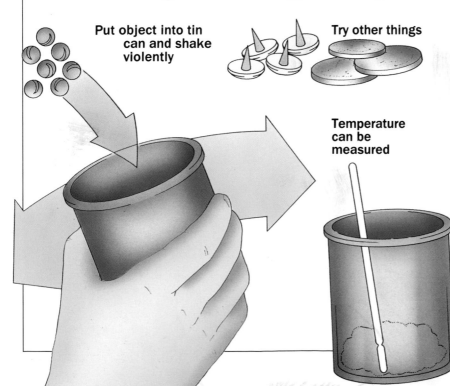

Put object into tin can and shake violently

Try other things

Temperature can be measured

QUIZ

A bicycle pump gets hot as it pumps. Energy squeezes air molecules into a small space. Why does the temperature increase? The energy is converted to heat.

There is a difference between heat and temperature. The heat of an object is the total amount of energy it has because its molecules are moving. Moving molecules have kinetic energy. The temperature of the object indicates how fast the molecules are moving. The faster they move, the higher the temperature.

TEMPERATURE SCALES

There are three common temperature scales: Celsius (which is the same thing as centigrade), Fahrenheit and kelvin. On the Celsius scale, the temperature of freezing water is 0°C, and the temperature of boiling water is 100°C. On the Fahrenheit scale, freezing water is 32°F and boiling water is 212°F. Zero degrees in the kelvin scale is taken as the lowest possible temperature, called absolute zero, which is -273.15°C (-459.67°F). The size of a degree in the kelvin scale is the same as in the Celsius scale. So freezing water is 273.15 K.

△ An iceberg contains more heat than a cup of boiling water. Even though it is freezing, it is large and so its total energy is enormous.

▽ The hottest place on Earth is Al'Aziziyah in Libya. On September 13, 1922, a temperature of 58°C (136.4°F) was recorded.

THERMOMETERS

There are many different kinds of thermometers. The simplest kind contains a liquid, such as mercury, which expands when heated. The expanding liquid moves up a thin glass tube marked with a scale. Other thermometers, called thermocouples, use metal strips that produce small amounts of electricity when heated. Another kind is a resistance thermometer. An electric current flowing through the thermometer varies as the temperature changes. A pyrometer compares the color of a hot object with that of an electrically-heated wire.

△ A pyrometer can be used to measure the very high temperature of a kiln.

Water freezes

Water boils

| 0 | 50 | 100 | 150 | 200 | 250 | 300 | 350 | 400 | 450 | KELVIN K |

| -273.15 | -200 | -150 | -100 | -50 | 0 | 50 | 100 | 150 | CELSIUS °C |

| -400 | -300 | -200 | -100 | 0 | 100 | 200 | 300 | | FAHRENHEIT °F |
| -459.67 | -350 | -250 | -150 | -50 | 50 | 150 | 250 | 350 | |

MAKE AN AIR THERMOMETER

To make a simple thermometer, you will need a small bottle with a tight-fitting cork with a hole through its center. Carefully push a piece of clear plastic tube through the hole. Fix the bottle with the tube dipping into some colored water. Put your hand on the bottle to warm it. Air will bubble from the bottom of the tube. When you remove your hand, water will rise up the tube. Put the thermometer in different places and watch the water level. Can you make a scale for your thermometer by fixing cardboard to the tube?

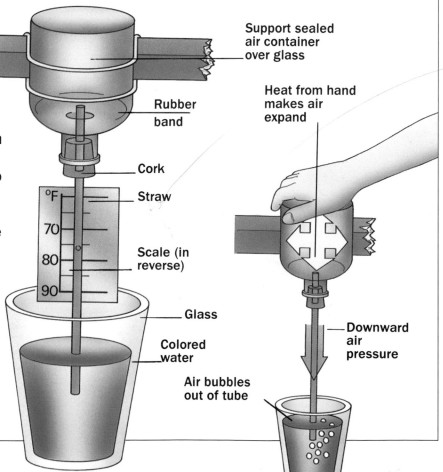

Support sealed air container over glass

Rubber band

Cork

Straw

Scale (in reverse)

Glass

Colored water

Air bubbles out of tube

Heat from hand makes air expand

Downward air pressure

The lowest temperatures on Earth occur in Antarctica. On July 21, 1983, the Soviet research station at Vostok recorded a temperature of -89.2°C (-128.6°F). The coldest place in the Solar System is Pluto. Its average temperature is -382°F. In outer space, away from any star, even lower temperatures occur: about -454°F.

HOW LOW CAN YOU GO?

As an object gets colder, its molecules move less and less quickly. If it were possible to continue the cooling process, the molecules would eventually become completely still. The temperature at which movement of molecules stops is called absolute zero (equal to -459.67°F, -273.15°C or 0 K). But at very low temperatures, it is extremely difficult to remove heat from an object. It is impossible to reach absolute zero exactly.

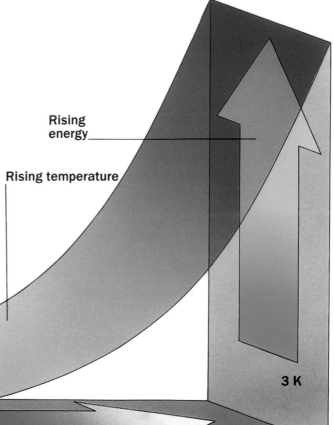

▽ At absolute zero, an object has no heat energy. But even just above absolute zero, its molecules start to vibrate, and it does have heat energy.

Rising energy

Rising temperature

0 K (absolute zero)

3 K

▽ Liquid hydrogen and oxygen are used to power space rockets. The hydrogen burns with the oxygen in the combustion chamber of the rocket motor.

Fuel lines

Combustion chamber

Nozzle

Liquid oxygen

LOW TEMPERATURE GASES

Many gases can be cooled until they become liquids. Oxygen and nitrogen can be liquified in this way. Liquid hydrogen and helium are produced in a two-stage cooling process in which they are compressed, cooled and then allowed to expand through a small nozzle to obtain further cooling. When a gas expands rapidly, it cools down. Liquid gases are very cold and can be used for a number of purposes. For example, they can be used in medicine to freeze some living tissues very quickly. The tissues are then not damaged by the freezing. Making gases into liquids can also be a way of storing them — for example, to use as rocket fuel.

SUPERFLUIDS AND CONDUCTORS

At temperatures near to absolute zero, some materials behave in strange ways. Certain metals, such as lead and mercury, lose their resistance to the passage of an electric current. They become superconductors. If an electric current starts to move through a superconductor, it keeps on flowing forever. Liquid helium also behaves strangely near absolute zero. It is a superfluid, and can flow uphill. If an empty cup is placed in a bowl of superfluid helium, the liquid climbs up the sides and fills the cup. If the bowl becomes empty, the liquid flows out of the cup and back into the bowl.

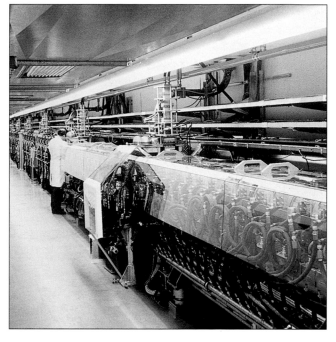

△ Superconductors can carry large currents and are used to make the very powerful magnets needed for particle accelerators.

Liquid hydrogen

▷ Superfluid helium crawls into an empty container, and then flows out again. If the helium is put into a powder-filled cone, it makes a fountain when flowing upward through the nozzle.

Liquid helium

Helium crawls into empty beaker

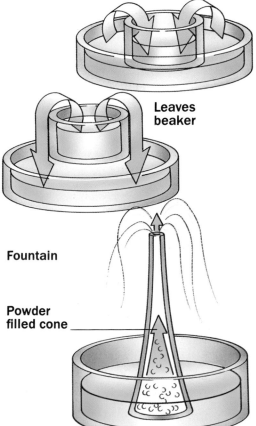

Leaves beaker

Fountain

Powder filled cone

The highest temperature of all time occurred about 15,000 million years ago, during the enormous explosion that began the Universe. This produced temperatures of at least 10 billion degrees. On Earth, temperatures are much lower. The hottest flame burns at about 9,032°F.

INSIDE THE STARS

The Sun is a star, and at its center the temperature is 15 million degrees. In the center of a star, matter is converted into energy by the process of nuclear fusion, in which small atoms join to make larger ones. The energy flows outward through the radiative layer as radiation. In the convective layer, currents of hot material carry the heat. The photosphere is a thin, relatively cool outer layer which glows — the Sun's photosphere is at 10,832°F. The outermost layer, the chromosphere, is a region with giant flames that leap thousands of miles into space.

△ The highest man-made temperatures are those that occur at the center of a nuclear bomb blast, where they can reach as high as 300-400 million degrees.

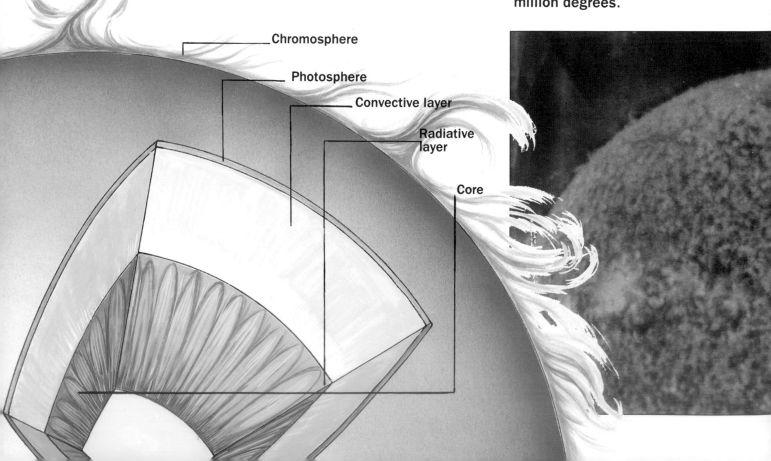

Chromosphere

Photosphere

Convective layer

Radiative layer

Core

INSIDE THE EARTH

The surface of the Earth is a thin layer of rock called the crust. It is about 5 mi thick under the sea and about 25 mi thick on land. Below the crust is a layer of liquid rock (magma) about 1,800 mi thick. This layer — called the mantle — has a temperature of 2,732-5,400°F. The molten rock sometimes flows through cracks in the crust or out of volcanoes, as lava. Beneath the mantle lies the outer core, composed of liquid metal at a temperature of 7,053°F. Finally, right at the center, is a ball of solid metal 1,700 mi across. Its temperature reaches as much as 7,200°F.

▽ Red-hot lava flows like a river from an erupting volcano. This molten rock has a temperature of up to 1,800°F.

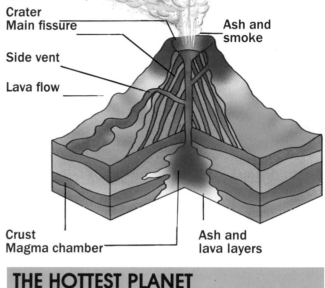

Crater
Main fissure
Side vent
Lava flow
Ash and smoke
Crust
Magma chamber
Ash and lava layers

THE HOTTEST PLANET

Mercury is the planet nearest the Sun. During the day, the temperature on Mercury reaches 660°F, which is more than six times hotter than the highest temperature recorded on Earth.

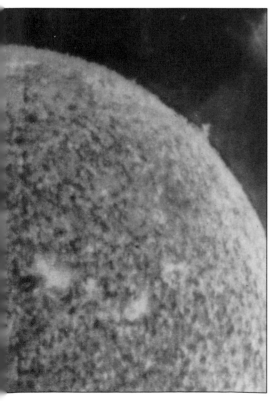

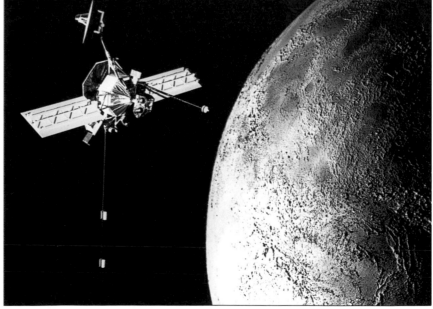

◁ Giant flames, called prominences, stream out from the Sun. The largest are nearly 40 times the size of the Earth.

△ The surface of Mercury is like that of the Moon: rocky, airless and waterless, with many meteorite craters.

Heat energy can move, and it can travel in three different ways: by radiation, convection or conduction. It travels through empty space as radiation, or heat rays. In gases and liquids, hot currents called convection currents carry the heat. And heat travels through solids, such as metals, by conduction.

HEAT RAYS

Heat rays are also called infrared radiation, because they are similar to light. Like light rays, they are electromagnetic waves that travel through space at great speed. Infrared radiation has a slightly longer wavelength than red light. Both light and infrared radiation travel at the same speed: nearly 186,000 miles per second. More infrared radiation is given out than absorbed by anything that is hotter than its surroundings. Cold objects absorb more infrared rays that fall on them than they emit. Dark colored objects absorb heat better than light colored ones.

FLOWING HEAT

When a gas, such as air, is heated by a candle, the heated air expands. The hot air becomes less dense than the cooler air around it, and so it rises. As the warm air rises, cooler air moves in to take its place. Soon a steady current of air is set up: warm air rises, carrying heat with it; when this air has cooled, it falls and is warmed again. These are convection currents. On a larger scale, convection currents take place in the atmosphere, causing winds. Air is heated by the Sun in a hot region, such as the tropics. The heated air rises and air flows in from colder regions to take its place. Convection currents carry heat in liquids as well as in gases. Peas in gently boiling water in a saucepan are carried to the surface by convection currents.

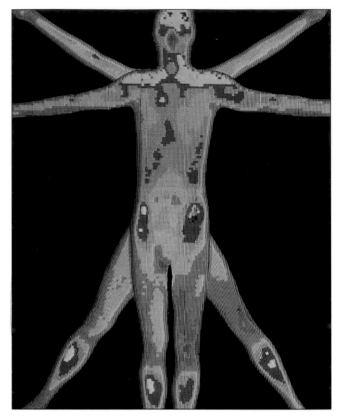

△ Doctors use special photographs taken using heat radiation to detect diseased tissues, which are usually warmer than healthy ones.

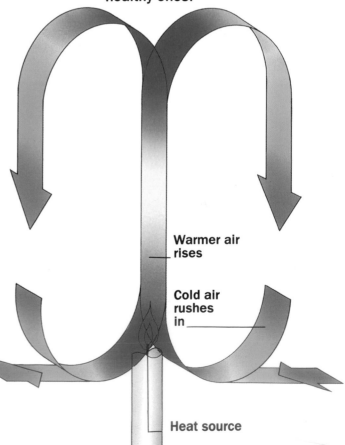

Warmer air rises

Cold air rushes in

Heat source

CONDUCTION

When one end of a metal bar is held in a candle flame, metal atoms near the flame get extra heat energy from it. They start to vibrate more rapidly, bumping into neighboring atoms and transferring energy to them. They in turn jostle their neighbors, and pass energy to them. This process, called conduction, carries heat energy along the bar. When you pick up a metal object, it often feels colder than it really is. This is because the heat of your fingers is conducted away rapidly by the metal. A poor conductor, such as a piece of cloth, does not feel cold.

Hot end
Much vibration

Cold end

Little vibration

Vibration transfers heat

Heat energy from flame

▽ Convection currents carry milk to the surface from the warm cup bottom. A spoon feels hot because it conducts heat from the liquid.

QUIZ

Why are houses in hot climates often painted white, and why is the Space Shuttle also white? Because light colors reflect most of the Sun's heat rays, while dark colors absorb them.

When a solid is heated, its atoms or molecules vibrate more rapidly. If the heating continues, some molecules start to move more freely, and the solid begins to melt. Eventually, it becomes a liquid. If the liquid is heated further, the molecules obtain enough energy to leap through the surface, and the liquid boils.

HIDDEN HEAT

While a liquid is boiling, its temperature stays the same even though it is being heated. The heat being supplied, rather than increasing the temperature of the liquid, is used to give molecules enough energy to escape from the surface and become a gas or vapor. The energy needed to turn a boiling liquid into a gas or vapor is called the latent, or hidden, heat because it does not cause a temperature rise.

△ In high mountain regions, the low air pressure allows water to boil at a temperature below its normal boiling point.

▽ A painrelief spray works by vaporizing rapidly. This extracts heat from the injured muscle and kills pain.

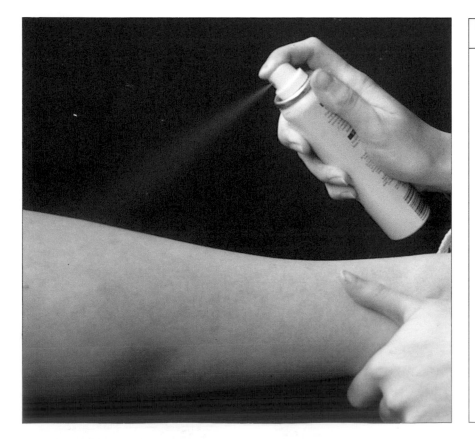

ICE TRICKS

Squeeze two ice cubes together. When you release the pressure, the cubes will have joined. This happens because the ice on the sides of the cubes that join melts when you apply pressure, and then it refreezes when the pressure is released. Next, hang a heavy weight over a cube of ice using metal wire or a thin piece of string. The wire will cut its way through the ice, which will refreeze when the wire has passed through.

MELTING AND BOILING POINTS

The melting point is the temperature at which a solid melts; the boiling point is the temperature at which a liquid boils. A pure substance at normal pressure always melts and boils at the same temperatures. But if the substance is impure, or the pressure is changed, the melting and boiling points change. Salt water boils at a higher temperature than pure water. Water boils at a lower temperature if the pressure is reduced.

△ Icicles form when dripping water freezes. The drips freeze along the icicle, which is why icicles get their pointed shape. As the temperature rises, the ice melts and the water starts to drip again.

◁ Dry ice is frozen carbon dioxide, which is a gas at room temperature. When it is warmed, it turns back into a gas without turning into a liquid first.

QUIZ

Why do cooks boil vegetables in salty water? The main reason is to improve the taste. But it also helps the food to cook more quickly. Why? Because salty water boils at a higher temperature than pure water.

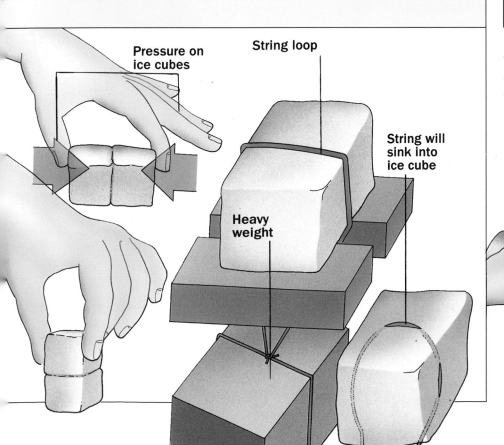

Pressure on ice cubes

String loop

String will sink into ice cube

Heavy weight

Some materials conduct heat more easily than others. Gases and liquids are poor conductors. Metals are good conductors, but some are better than others. Copper conducts heat three times better than iron or steel, 1,000 times better than glass and 10,000 times better than air. Poor conductors are called insulators.

KEEPING WARM

Woolen clothes keep us warm because they trap a layer of air. The air is an insulator, so heat cannot easily escape through it. For the same reason, polar explorers wear several layers of clothing, rather than a single thick garment, because more air is trapped in this way. Glass fiber, a poor conductor of heat itself, traps air and is used to insulate house attics. A thermos uses a double-walled glass bottle to keep hot liquids hot (or cold liquids cold). The space between the walls is a vacuum, so that no heat can be conducted across. The walls are silvered to prevent radiation — the mirrorlike surfaces reflect radiant heat. The bottle is insulated from its container.

△ A sheep's wool traps air and keeps the animal warm, just as clothing made out of wool keeps its human wearer warm.

▽ Glass fiber is a good attic insulator because it traps a layer of air. It is also put into walls to prevent heat loss.

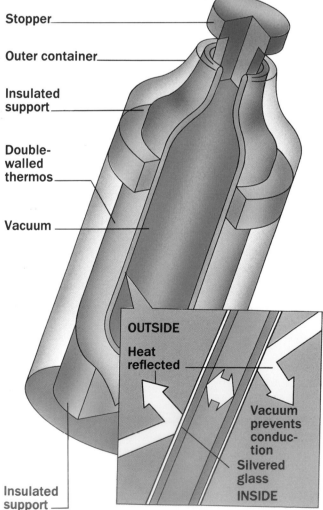

Stopper

Outer container

Insulated support

Double-walled thermos

Vacuum

Insulated support

OUTSIDE

Heat reflected

Vacuum prevents conduction

Silvered glass

INSIDE

COOLERS

Insulators can help to keep things cold. Houses built with well-insulated walls are cool in summer, as well as warm in winter, because heat cannot pass through the walls. In a car's cooling system, water is circulated around the hot engine to carry away unwanted heat. The water flows through thin pipes in a radiator. Cool air drawn in by a fan flows over these pipes, cooling the water.

In a refrigerator, a liquid called the refrigerant evaporates to form a gas in the pipes around the freezer. The heat needed for evaporation is absorbed from the inside of the freezer. A compressor then changes the gas back into a liquid. This process produces heat, which is released into the air by a radiator at the back of the refrigerator.

THE REFRIGERATOR

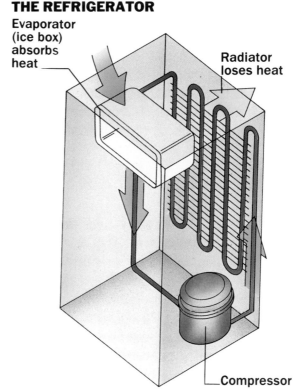

Evaporator (ice box) absorbs heat

Radiator loses heat

Compressor

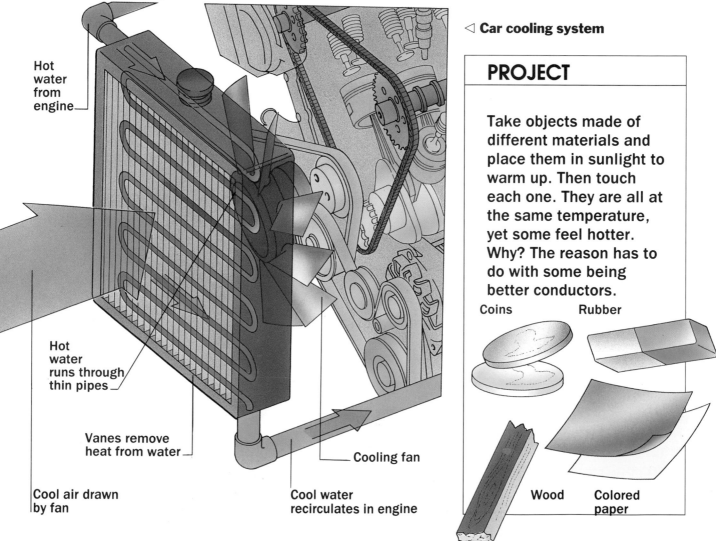

◁ **Car cooling system**

Hot water from engine

Hot water runs through thin pipes

Vanes remove heat from water

Cool air drawn by fan

Cooling fan

Cool water recirculates in engine

PROJECT

Take objects made of different materials and place them in sunlight to warm up. Then touch each one. They are all at the same temperature, yet some feel hotter. Why? The reason has to do with some being better conductors.

Coins

Rubber

Wood

Colored paper

Almost all materials expand (get bigger) when heated. This is because the atoms or molecules that make up the material move more vigorously as temperature increases. They, therefore, take up more room, and the material expands. When a hot object cools down, it contracts (gets smaller) and returns to its original size.

EVERYDAY EXPANSION

There are many everyday examples of expansion and contraction. On a hot day, overhead telephone wires or power lines hang slackly. On a cold winter day, the wires contract and stretch tightly between the poles. Railroads are built with angled gaps between lengths of rail, so that the rails do not buckle when they expand in summer. The supersonic airliner Concorde heats up during flight because of friction with the air; it grows up to 10 inches longer.

△ A large suspension bridge may be up to three feet longer in summer than in winter. Gaps are left in the road for expansion.

RAIL EXPANSION JOINT
Angled gap allows motion

Bracket allows motion only along length

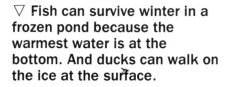

▽ Fish can survive winter in a frozen pond because the warmest water is at the bottom. And ducks can walk on the ice at the surface.

FROZEN WATER

Water behaves very strangely when it is cooled to near its freezing temperature. Above 39°F it contracts when cooled. But when cooled below this temperature, water expands, so that between 32°F and 39°F water is less dense than warmer water and floats on top of it. In winter, the colder water is in a layer on top, which is why the surface of a pond freezes first. This is extremely important for fish and other water life. The ice protects the water below it from freezing air, and the warmest water is on the bottom, where the fish stay during winter.

THE THERMOSTAT

Thermostats are switches that turn on at a certain temperature, and turn off at another, higher, temperature. They are used to control electric cookers and heaters. The heart of a thermostat is a bimetallic strip, which is made from two strips of different metals sandwiched together. When the bimetallic strip heats up, it bends because one metal expands more than the other. If the strip is part of an electrical circuit, the circuit is broken as the strip bends and this switches off the current. When the temperature falls, the bimetallic strip bends back and reconnects the current.

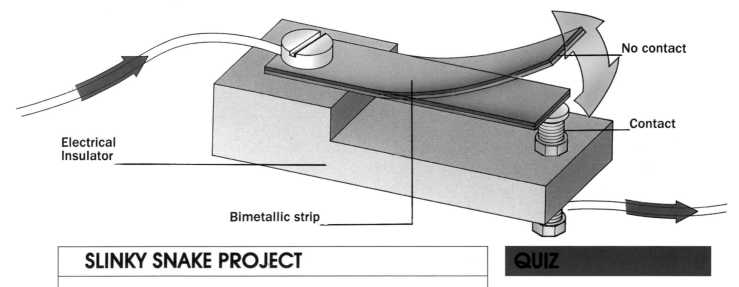

No contact

Contact

Electrical Insulator

Bimetallic strip

SLINKY SNAKE PROJECT

This project shows how metals expand. First, put a strip of transparent sticky tape on a piece of aluminum foil. Next, cut a snake from the foil, with the tape running along the snake's body.

Coil the snake by wrapping it around a pencil. Put the coiled snake under a table lamp, where the heat of the lamp will warm it. The snake will uncoil as the foil expands.

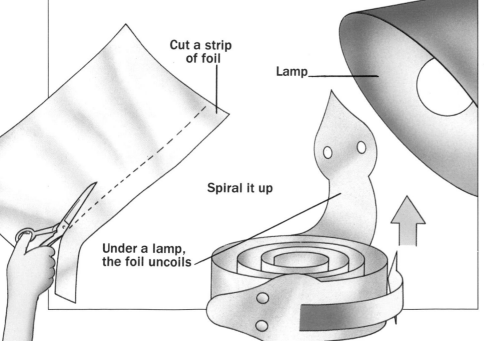

Cut a strip of foil

Lamp

Spiral it up

Under a lamp, the foil uncoils

QUIZ

If you float an ice cube in a glass full to the brim with water, what will happen as the ice melts? Will the water spill out of the glass? No, because the ice occupies more volume than the water it turns into when it melts.

Burning is a chemical reaction or change — a change that produces a new substance and is hard to reverse. Many chemical changes need heat or another form of energy to get started, and many also produce heat. In striking a match, for example, friction against the box produces enough heat to light it.

OXYGEN AND BURNING

The chemical reaction in burning is between the substance being burned — the fuel — and oxygen in the air. It releases energy because the molecules of the fuel are full of energy. The burning process breaks these energy-packed molecules into different low-energy molecules. For instance, when coal burns, carbon in the coal combines with oxygen in the air to form carbon dioxide. Natural gas is mostly methane; it burns to produce carbon dioxide and water.

▷ When methane burns, its molecules combine with oxygen molecules to produce carbon dioxide and water.

Carbon dioxide (CO_2)

Water (steam, H_2O)

Methane (CH_4)

Oxygen (O_2)

EXPERIMENTS

You can estimate the amount of oxygen in air. Ask an adult to supervise this experiment. Put a candle on a tinfoil "boat" floating in a bowl of water and light the candle (a short candle will balance more easily). Lower a large jar over the candle and the tinfoil. At first, the water does not enter the jar; the air in the jar keeps it out. As the oxygen is used up by the burning candle, the water rises in the jar. When all the oxygen is gone and the candle goes out, estimate the fraction of air left in the jar.

Lower jam jar over candle

Burning candle in tinfoil container

Bowl of water

Air pressure forces out water

Candle burns oxygen

Water sucked into jar

FUELS

Most of the fuels we use are fossil fuels: coal, oil, and natural gas. They are called fossil fuels because they were formed long ago from the remains of plants and animals. Coal was formed from giant plants that grew on Earth about 300 million years ago. Oil and gas were formed from the remains of algae and other small plants that lived in the sea millions of years ago. All of these fuels contain carbon and so, when they burn, they produce carbon dioxide. Over the last 100 years, the amount of carbon dioxide made from burning fuels has increased. Scientists think that this will cause the atmosphere to warm up like the air in a greenhouse.

◁ Smoke from a power station contains chemicals that cause the atmosphere to warm up.

FIRE FIGHTING

A fire needs three things to start and keep going: heat, fuel, and oxygen. If any of these is missing, the fire goes out. If the doors and windows of a burning building are closed, the fire might be starved of oxygen and go out. Water sprayed onto a fire puts it out by removing heat or cooling the burning material. If somebody's clothes are on fire, wrapping them in a blanket cuts off oxygen and puts out the flames.

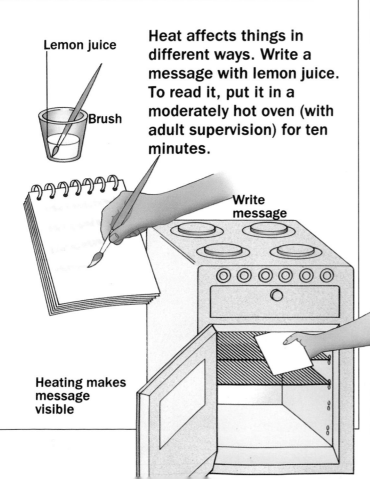

Heat affects things in different ways. Write a message with lemon juice. To read it, put it in a moderately hot oven (with adult supervision) for ten minutes.

Lemon juice

Brush

Write message

Heating makes message visible

△ A fire fighter uses foam to blanket a burning aircraft, so cutting off oxygen and putting out the fire.

Gunpowder is a mixture of carbon, sulfur and a chemical called saltpeter, which contains oxygen. When gunpowder explodes, the carbon and sulfur burn, using the oxygen in the saltpeter. A different process, respiration, takes place in living things. It is a form of slow burning that releases energy from food.

EXPLOSIVES

There are two kinds of explosives, called low and high. A low explosive, such as gunpowder, burns relatively slowly and produces a weak explosion. A high explosive burns extremely quickly and produces a very powerful blast. Dynamite, made from nitroglycerine, is the best-known high explosive. Another high explosive is TNT (trinitrotoluene), which is easier to make and handle.

FIREWORKS

Fireworks are made from gunpowder and other substances that produce special effects such as colored flames and sparks. Green colors are given by substances containing barium, blue colors by copper compounds, and red colors by strontium salts. Sparks are formed by burning finely powdered steel, iron and aluminum. All these substances are packed into a cardboard tube or cone, with a paper lighting fuse at the top. In a Roman candle, for instance, the tube contains small packets called stars, which give out lots of colored sparks when they burn. The stars are separated by layers of gunpowder. The candle burns down until a star is reached. As it starts to burn, the gunpowder explodes, throwing the star high into the air.

△ The first safe high explosive, dynamite, was invented by the chemist Alfred Nobel. Here it is being used to demolish a tower block.

▷ The Chinese first made fireworks around 2,000 years ago, soon after they invented gunpowder. But fireworks then were not as spectacular as these.

ENERGY FOR LIFE

All living things need energy. They get it from energy-rich foods called carbohydrates, which are substances that contain hydrogen and carbon (such as sugars). A plant makes these foods for itself by absorbing carbon dioxide from the air and converting it by photosynthesis. Animals either eat plants to obtain carbohydrate foods, or eat other animals. Animals can also use fats and even proteins for energy. But an animal has to convert them into carbohydrates before using them. The energy held in foods is released by respiration, which is similar to burning. Respiration involves a complicated series of chemical changes, but the overall result is that oxygen combines with food substances to produce carbon dioxide, water and energy.

▽ Doctors test athletes to see how they react to vigorous exercise. Their fitness depends partly on how well they take in oxygen when they breathe.

FLAMING SUGAR CUBE

Put a sugar cube on an ashtray. Ask an adult to set fire to the cube: the sugar will not burn. Now rub a little ash onto the cube, and the cube will burn. The ash contains a catalyst, which is a substance that speeds up a chemical reaction.

There are two main kinds of engines: external combustion engines in which the fuel is burned outside the engine, and internal combustion engines in which the fuel is burned inside it. A steam engine is an external combustion engine; a gasoline or diesel engine is an internal combustion engine.

STEAM ENGINE

The first steam engines were huge machines. In 1712, the British engineer Thomas Newcomen built a vertical engine that was 33 feet tall. Then in 1782 the Scotsman James Watt invented the double-acting steam engine. Steam was fed into one end of a cylinder, where a tight-fitting piston was pushed along by the steam pressure. The piston was connected by a rod to a wheel, and sideways movement of the piston caused the wheel to turn. When the piston reached the end of the cylinder, a sliding valve let steam in front of the piston and forced it back again.

GASOLINE ENGINE

The usual car engine is called a four-stroke engine. This is because it works in four movements, called strokes, of the pistons. During the first stroke, the piston moves down. At the top of the cylinder, a valve opens to let in a mixture of gasoline and air. On the second stroke, the piston moves up to compress the fuel-air mixture. When the mixture is fully compressed, a spark plug ignites the mixture with a small electric spark. The mixture burns, and the expanding gases drive the piston downward. This is the third stroke. The piston then moves up again, forcing the burned mixture out of the cylinder through the exhaust valve. A diesel engine works in a similar way, but has no spark plug; compression of the fuel is enough to ignite it.

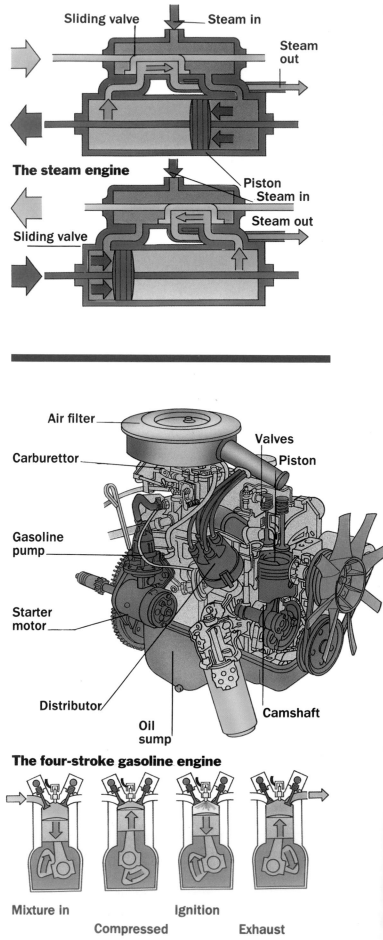

The steam engine

Sliding valve — Steam in — Steam out — Piston — Steam in — Steam out — Sliding valve

Air filter — Carburettor — Gasoline pump — Starter motor — Distributor — Oil sump — Valves — Piston — Camshaft

The four-stroke gasoline engine

Mixture in — Compressed — Ignition — Exhaust

TURBINES

A turbine consists of a wheel with blades — like a small windmill — mounted on a shaft. The wheel is made to turn by a stream of water, steam or hot gas flowing over the blades. In steam turbines, high-pressure steam flows over the blades. Often a series of steam turbines is used in power stations. In a gas turbine, also called a jet engine, air is drawn into the front of the turbine and compressed by fans connected to the turbine shaft. The compressed air passes into a combustion chamber where a fuel, such as kerosene, is burned. The hot gases produced expand and flow through the drive fans before passing out of the engine as a high-speed exhaust. The drive fans make the compressor fans turn. If the turbine is being used to work machinery, the turbine shaft is connected to the machinery. In gas turbine driven ships, the shaft is connected to the propeller. Jet engines in airplanes are also a sort of gas turbine, but it is the hot exhaust that makes the airplane move.

▽ Power stations use huge steam turbines. The shaft turns so fast that the tips of the blades move faster than sound.

△ The fans at the front of an airliner engine draw in air. They are turned by a drive fan at the back of the engine.

TO CREATE POWER

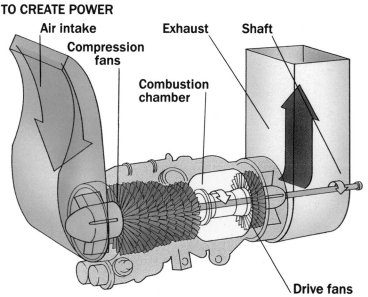

Air intake

Compression fans

Exhaust

Shaft

Combustion chamber

Drive fans

▷ A gas turbine engine can create large amounts of power, but it also creates large amounts of hot exhaust.

Heat has many uses in industry. For example, it is used for extracting metals from their ores. Iron is produced by heating iron ore in a blast furnace with coke. The ore is usually hematite, which contains iron and oxygen. Coke is mainly carbon, made by roasting coal. The resulting pig iron is used to make steel.

SHAPING UP

Hot materials are easy to bend and form into various shapes. This is why a blacksmith heats a horseshoe to red heat before hammering it into shape. This method of shaping a metal is called forging. Some car engine parts are made by forging. Casting is another way of shaping metals. Molten metal is poured into a mold and left to cool. Wheels for railroad cars are made by casting. Molten glass or plastic can also be molded, or blown into hollow shapes. Other plastic shapes are made by extrusion, which involves squeezing them through a specially shaped hole.

△ Molten pig iron can be poured into molds to make ingots. It can also be cast into more complicated shapes.

▽ Large pieces of hot metal can be forged into shape by using very powerful hydraulic hammers or presses.

◁ A glass worker blows air into the center of a molten glass ball, expanding the glass to form a bottle.

AT AN OIL REFINERY

Many useful substances can be made from crude oil, or petroleum. The first step is to heat it, causing it to boil off gases. The gases pass into a tall distillation column. As the gases pass up the column and cool, they change into liquids that collect on the trays set across the column. Different liquids — called fractions — collect on different trays and are drawn off through pipes. The lightest fractions with the lowest boiling points are drawn off at the top of the column. They include butane and propane. Lower down, gasoline, kerosene and fuel oils are produced. Heavy black bitumen, or tar, is left at the bottom.

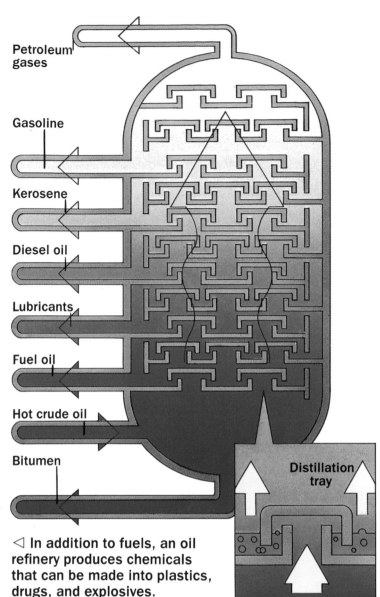

Petroleum gases
Gasoline
Kerosene
Diesel oil
Lubricants
Fuel oil
Hot crude oil
Bitumen

Distillation tray
Rising gas

◁ In addition to fuels, an oil refinery produces chemicals that can be made into plastics, drugs, and explosives.

PROJECT

Fill a glass halfway with warm water and put a mark on the side to show the level. Stirring the water, mix in as much salt as will dissolve. Does the water level rise? Where does the salt go? Next pour some of the salt solution onto a saucer, and put it in sunlight. After a while, the water will evaporate, leaving behind small salt crystals.

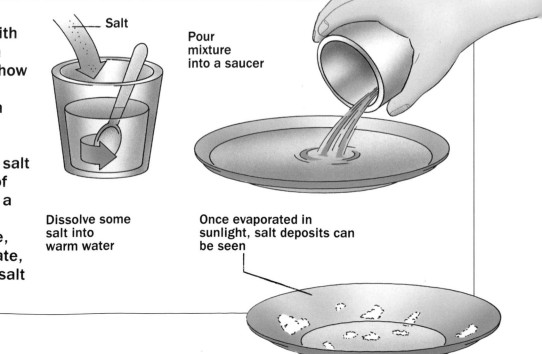

Salt

Dissolve some salt into warm water

Pour mixture into a saucer

Once evaporated in sunlight, salt deposits can be seen

The scientific understanding of heat and how to make use of it has depended on the work of many scientists. A few have been especially important, and there are pictures of three of them here.

Lord Kelvin (1824-1907) was a British scientist, born in Belfast. He was the first person to suggest using a temperature scale that started at absolute zero. This scale is now named after him: the kelvin scale. This scale is important because it is based on the total amount of heat energy that an object has in it.

Lord Kelvin

James Prescott Joule

Kelvin could not have done his work without the ideas of James Prescott Joule (1818-1889). Joule showed that heat is a form of energy. It is said that he measured the temperature of the water at the top and at the bottom of a waterfall to test his ideas. Then, in his laboratory, he made more exact measurements of the amount of heat produced by a certain amount of mechanical energy. He did this by using falling weights to drive paddle wheels inside a container of water, and measuring the temperature rise of the water. The unit for measuring amounts of heat energy (and other sorts of energy) is named after him: the joule.

Joseph Black (1728-1799) was a Scottish scientist. He noticed that ice can melt without changing its temperature. This meant that ice could absorb heat and use the energy to change into a liquid. He then discovered that the same

thing happens when water turns into steam. The energy that is absorbed when a substance changes from a solid to a liquid is the latent heat of fusion; and when it changes from a liquid to a gas, it is the latent heat of vaporization. He also realized that the same amounts of different substances need to absorb different amounts of heat to rise by the same temperature.

Joseph Black

Absolute zero lowest possible temperature; it is -273.15°C or 0 K.

Atom smallest particle of an element; atoms combine with each other to form molecules.

Boiling point temperature at which a liquid changes into a gas or vapor.

Catalyst substance that speeds up a chemical reaction, but remains unchanged at the end of it.

Celsius temperature scale temperature scale on which the freezing point of water is 0° and the boiling point of water is 100°. It is the same as the centigrade temperature scale. The degrees are the same size as those on the kelvin temperature scale.

Electromagnetic wave wave that can travel through empty space. Light and heat rays travel as electromagnetic waves.

Energy ability to do work. It can be measured in joules.

Fahrenheit temperature scale temperature scale on which the freezing point of water is 32° and the boiling point of water is 212°.

Internal combustion engine engine in which the fuel is burned inside the engine, such as a gasoline engine or a diesel engine.

Joule unit that is used to measure amounts of energy. One joule is the energy needed to lift a weight of one newton a distance of three feet.

Kelvin temperature scale temperature scale on which absolute zero is 0 and the freezing point of water is 273.15. The degrees on this scale are the same size as those on the Celsius temperature scale.

Kinetic energy energy that a moving object has because it is moving.

Latent heat amount of heat absorbed when a liquid boils, or a solid melts.

Melting point temperature at which a solid turns into a liquid.

Molecule small particle of matter that consists of atoms joined together.

Potential energy stored energy, such as that in a stretched spring or a weight raised above the ground.

Power rate of doing work, measured in watts (joules per second).

Radiation energy that can pass through empty space. Heat travels through empty space as infrared radiation.

Refrigerant liquid that circulates through the working parts of a refrigerator and evaporates to produce cooling.

Respiration process by which living things produce energy from food substances — especially carbohydrates.

Sublimation process in which a solid changes directly into a gas without first becoming a liquid.

Vibration rapid back-and-forth movement. The molecules of a substance vibrate more rapidly when heated.

Watt unit used to measure power. One watt equals one joule per second.

Photographic Credits:
Cover and pages 13 top two, 18 both, 20 top and 22: Spectrum Colour Library; pages 4, 7 bottom, 9 top, 12, 16 top middle, 24 top, 26 bottom, and 28 bottom three: Robert Harding Library; pages 6, 7 top, 9 middle, 14 bottom, 20 bottom, 24 top, 26 top and 28 top: J Allan Cash Library; page 9 bottom: Eye Ubiquitous; pages 10, 13 bottom, 14 top and 16 middle bottom: Science Photo Library; page 11: Professor Allen, University of St Andrews; pages 14 middle and 16 top: Roger Vlitos; page 16 bottom: Topham Picture Library; page 30 all: Mansell Collection.

PRINTED IN BELGIUM BY
proost
INTERNATIONAL BOOK PRODUCTION